JUST add MILK

EXTRAORDINARY COOKIES FOR THE EVERYDAY BAKER

RECIPES BY
LORIE JOHNSON AND
KRISTEN JOHNSON-SLATE

PHOTOGRAPHY BY
LISA MURPHY PHOTOGRAPHY
LISAMURPHYPHOTOGRAPHY.COM

DESIGNED BY
KRISTEN SLATE DESIGN

KRISTENSLATEDESIGN.COM

TABLE *of* CONTENTS

SEASONAL *66*

ORANGE SUGARS with CHOCOLATE GANACHE

CRANBERRY + ORANGE + WHITE CHOCOLATE

CHEESECAKE STUFFED PUMPKIN DOODLES

SUGAR COOKIES with BUTTERCREAM FROSTING

CHOCOLATE LINZERS with DULCE DE LECHE

CHOCOLATE WAFFLE IRON COOKIES

SCANDINAVIAN ALMOND COOKIES

ANGEL FOOD COOKIES

PEANUT BUTTER BLOSSOMS

GINGER MOLASSES

PEPPERMINT CRACKLES

SPICY GINGERBREAD

EGGNOG COOKIES

RED VELVET

SHORTBREAD *94*

BROWN SUGAR SHORTIES

CHOCOLATE ESPRESSO

LAVENDER THINS

FRUITS + NUTS + GRAINS *100*

ROSEMARY + WALNUT COOKIES

NO BAKE BIRD SEED MOUNDS

CHOCOLATE CHIP OATIES

CARAMELIZED APPLE OATMEAL

JUMBO SALTED PEANUT COOKIE

RASPBERRY ALMOND THUMBPRINTS

ALMOND BUTTER COOKIE

MACADAMIA NUT + BLUEBERRY

COCONUT KEY LIME

TRAIL MIXERS

SAUCES *120*

SALTED CARAMEL SAUCE

CHOCOLATE SAUCE

CHOCOLATE ESPRESSO SAUCE

FROM OUR BAKING SHEETS
TO YOURS.

Just Add Milk is a collaborative family project between three generations of bakers, with a love for one dessert amongst all others—cookies! This passion project has been in the works for several years and has finally culminated into something that can now be shared with baking enthusiasts of all experience levels.

Many traditional cookie recipes are featured here; some with up to date modifications, along with current trending recipes and seasonal favorites. These recipes are the center of precious moments and long lasting memories that we hold dear to our hearts and now, have the honor of sharing with you.

My mother, Lorie had baked with her mom as a young child and then began to take an interest in cake decorating in college. People quickly realized her talent, making beautiful cakes that also tasted delicious; she opened a business called Cake Creations in Bozeman, Montana which was established in 1994.

When I was a little girl, my mother encouraged me to join her in the bakery to learn the tricks of her trade. However, it wasn't until years later that I realized that the creativity in my current profession, graphic design, could also be applied to baking. Years passed and I inevitably acquired the talent and enjoyment for this skill and have found my own niche in the business world, combining both services.

Much like this project, baking is a labor of love and when you share the cookies that you've made with friends and family, that thoughtfulness and hard work will be apparent. Let us help get you started on making sweet memories of your own in the kitchen with *Just Add Milk*.

Spread the love... BAKE COOKIES!
Happy Holidays, ♥ Kh

CLASSIC CHOCOLATE CHIP

½ cup margarine

½ cup shortening

¼ cup vegetable oil

1 ½ cups granulated sugar

1 ½ cups packed brown sugar

3 eggs

1 ½ tsp. baking soda

3 tsp. vanilla

1 ½ tsp. salt

3 cups all–purpose flour

1 ½ cups semi–sweet chocolate chips

Preheat oven to 350 degrees and line a baking sheet with a non–stick baking mat.

Using an electric mixer, cream together margarine, shortening, vegetable oil and both sugars.

Add eggs in one by one as the mixer continues to blend the ingredients; mixture will be slightly lumpy.

Add baking soda, vanilla and salt and mix together for another minute or two.

With the mixer on low speed, carefully add flour, one cup at a time and stir until all ingredients are combined evenly.

With a spatula or spoon, gently fold in chocolate chips.

Drop spoonfuls of dough onto the prepared sheets and bake cookies for 10 to12 minutes or until golden brown.

Remove carefully from baking sheet and transfer to cooling rack.

CRUNCHY PEANUT BUTTER

1 cup shortening
1 cup packed brown sugar
1 cup granulated sugar
2 eggs
1 cup crunchy peanut butter
1 tsp. cream of tartar
1 tsp. baking soda
(dissolved in 1 Tbsp. water)
½ tsp. salt
2½ cups all-purpose flour
sugar for sprinkling

Preheat oven to 350 degrees and line a baking sheet with a non-stick baking mat.

Cream together shortening, sugars and eggs until mostly smooth. Then add peanut butter, cream of tartar, salt and baking soda/water and mix again.

Add flour and mix until all ingredients are evenly distributed. Scoop out small spoonfuls of dough, roll into balls and place onto the baking sheet.

With the palm of your hand, flatten the ball down to make a thick disc and make a criss cross indentation with the back of a fork. Sprinkle with granulated sugar.

Bake for 10 to 12 minutes or until the edges of each cookie are slightly browned and transfer the cookies to a cooling rack immediately.

BIRTHDAY CAKE
with SPRINKLES

½ cup vegetable oil
1 box vanilla cake mix
1 tsp. baking powder
2 eggs
½ tsp. vanilla
1 cup sprinkles

Preheat oven to 350 degrees and line a baking sheet with a non-stick baking mat.

In a large bowl, mix together all ingredients except for the sprinkles. Beat the dough to break apart the cake mix.

Once the dough is smooth, fold in sprinkles but do not to over mix or the colors of the sprinkles will bleed into the dough.

Drop rounded balls of dough onto the prepared baking sheet and bake for 8 to 10 minutes. Be sure not to let cookies brown at all.

Remove from the oven and allow cookies to set up and cool.

OATMEAL RAISIN

¾ cup margarine

½ cup shortening

1 cup granulated sugar

1 cup loosely packed brown sugar

3 eggs

1½ tsp. baking soda

1½ tsp. cinnamon

1½ tsp. vanilla

¾ tsp. baking powder

¾ tsp. salt

4½ cups old-fashioned oats

1¾ cup all-purpose flour

1¾ cup raisins

Preheat oven to 325 degrees and line a baking sheet with a non-stick baking mat.

With an electric mixer, cream the sugars and shortenings together, then add vanilla and eggs and blend until smooth.

Add in all dry ingredients and mix well, then fold in the raisins.

Drop small spoonfuls of dough onto the prepared baking sheet and flatten down slightly.

Bake for 14 to 16 minutes and transfer cookies directly to cooling rack.

BROWN BUTTER
CHOCOLATE CHIP

10 Tbsp. unsalted butter, softened

½ cup vegetable oil

1 cup packed brown sugar

½ cup granulated sugar

2 eggs

2 Tbsp. whole milk, room temperature

3 tsp. vanilla

2¼ cups all–purpose flour

¾ cup bread flour

1 tsp. baking powder

½ tsp. baking soda

1 tsp. sea salt

2½ cups semi–sweet chocolate chips

Preheat oven to 375 degrees and line a baking sheet with a non-stick baking mat.

Put butter in a small saucepan and melt over medium heat. When the butter has completely melted, increase heat to medium high. Continue to stir and look for small golden bits that will begin to form. Once you see this, remove butter from the heat and set aside to cool for 5 to 10 minutes.

Whisk the brown sugar, granulated sugar, and oil into the cooled butter until smooth. Add in eggs one at a time, completely mixing in the first before adding the second. Whisk in the milk and vanilla until blended.

In a medium bowl, whisk together both flours, baking powder, baking soda, and sea salt. Add the flour mixture to the brown butter mixture and stir well, then fold in the chocolate chips.

Gently roll dough into 2 inch balls. Place the dough balls onto the prepared baking sheet about 2 inches apart. Sprinkle each with a pinch of sea salt.

Bake for 8 to 10 minutes. Let cool for 5 to 10 minutes on the baking sheet, then transfer the cookies to a cooling rack.

BANANA CREAM
PUDDING COOKIES

1 cup unsalted butter, softened

¾ cup loosely packed brown sugar

¼ cup granulated sugar

3.4 oz. package banana cream
instant pudding mix

2 eggs

1 tsp. vanilla

2¼ cups all–purpose flour

1 tsp. baking soda

½ tsp. salt

2 cups white chocolate chips

Preheat oven to 350 degrees and line a baking sheet with a non–stick baking mat.

In a large bowl mix together flour, baking soda, salt, and banana cream pudding mix then set aside.

In an electric mixer, cream together butter, sugars, vanilla and eggs.

Add in all dry ingredients and mix together until thoroughly combined. Gently fold in white chocolate chips.

Drop small spoonfuls of dough onto the prepared baking sheet and bake for 10 minutes or until slightly golden brown.

Remove cookies from the baking sheet and place onto a rack to cool.

M&M COOKIES

1 cup shortening
1 cup packed brown sugar
½ cup granulated sugar
2 eggs
1 tsp. baking soda
1 tsp. salt
1½ tsp. vanilla
2½ cups all-purpose flour
1 cup M&M candies

Preheat oven to 350 degrees and line a baking sheet with a non-stick baking mat.

Cream together shortening, sugars, eggs and vanilla until somewhat smooth.

Then add in flour, salt, baking soda and mix until all ingredients are incorporated.

Gently stir in M&M candies by hand and drop spoonfuls onto the prepared baking sheet.

Bake for 8 to 10 minutes, or until lightly golden brown. Remove from the baking sheet and transfer to a cooling rack.

SPICED RAISIN

1 cup shortening
1½ cups packed brown sugar
3 eggs, beaten
2¼ to 2½ cups all-purpose flour
1 tsp. baking soda
1 tsp. baking powder
1 tsp. cinnamon
1 tsp. vanilla
1 cup raisins

Preheat oven to 375 degrees and line a baking sheet with a non-stick baking mat.

Place raisins in a small saucepan and cover them with water. Bring water to a boil, then drain the raisins and set them aside to cool.

Cream the sugars and shortening together until light and fluffy, then add vanilla and eggs.

Add in dry ingredients and mix well. Stir in cooked and softened raisins.

Drop by spoonfuls onto the baking sheet and bake for 10 to 12 minutes.

Remove from baking sheet and place onto cooling rack.

CLASSIC MACAROONS

2 cups sweetened shredded coconut
14 oz. can sweetened condensed milk
1 tsp. vanilla
2 egg whites, at room temperature
¼ tsp. salt
¾ cup mini chocolate chips (optional)

Preheat oven to 325 degrees and line a baking sheet with a non-stick baking mat.

Combine the coconut, condensed milk and vanilla in a large bowl and stir.

With an electric mixer and whisk attachment, whip the egg whites and salt on high speed until medium-firm peaks have formed.

Carefully fold the egg whites into the coconut mixture. Shape mounds of dough onto the prepared baking sheet.

Bake for 25 to 30 minutes, until golden brown, then carefully transfer the cookies onto a cooling rack and let them set up.

FIVE POUNDER
(AL'S RECIPE)

¾ cup crunchy peanut butter

½ cup margarine

½ cup granulated sugar

1 cup packed brown sugar

3 eggs

1 tsp. vanilla

1 ½ tsp. baking soda

3 cups quick oatmeal

1 cup all—purpose flour

¼ cup semi—sweet chocolate chips

½ cup mini Reese's peanut butter cups

¼ cup butterscotch chips

1 ¼ cups M&M candies

Preheat oven to 350 degrees and line a baking sheet with a non-stick baking mat.

Cream together peanut butter, margarine, eggs, vanilla and sugars. Add in baking soda, flour and oatmeal, then stir.

Gently fold in all candies by hand. Drop heaping spoonfuls of dough onto the prepared sheet and bake 15 to 18 minutes or until cookies are golden brown and the center has set up.

Remove from the oven and let cookies cool for 5 minutes on the baking sheet. Once they have set up slightly, transfer them to a cooling rack.

SWEET ALMOND
BUTTER COOKIE

½ cup sweet cream butter, softened
½ cup powdered sugar
¼ cup ground almonds
+ ½ cup ground almonds for coating
1 egg
1 tsp. vanilla
1 cup all-purpose flour
pinch of salt

Preheat oven to 325 degrees and line a baking sheet with a non-stick baking mat.

Cream together butter, egg and powdered sugar, then add vanilla, salt and flour and mix again.

Add in ¼ cup ground almonds and mix until ingredients are evenly distributed.

Make one inch sized dough balls and roll each into the remaining ½ cup of ground almonds. Place onto the prepared baking sheet and gently flatten into thick discs.

Bake for 8 to 10 minutes until golden brown and carefully transfer the cookies onto a cooling rack.

TRADITIONAL DATE
FILLED COOKIES

Dough:
¼ cup salted butter, softened
¼ cup shortening
½ cup granulated sugar
½ cup lightly packed brown sugar
1 eggs
½ cup milk
1 tsp. vanilla
½ tsp. salt
2 tsp. cream of tartar
1 tsp. baking soda
dissolved in a little hot water
3¼ cups to 3½ cups all–purpose flour
turbinado sugar, for sprinkling

Date Filling:
2 cups pitted and chopped dates
½ cup brown sugar
2 Tbsp. all–purpose flour
1 cup water

For date filling, add all ingredients together in a small saucepan over low to medium heat and cook until mixture is thick (stir often as this burns easily). As soon as the mixture thickens, remove it from the heat and set aside to cool.

Preheat oven to 400 degrees and line a baking sheet with a non–stick baking mat.

With an electric mixer, cream together sugar, butter and shortening, then add the rest of the dough ingredients and mix. If dough is sticky, a little more flour may be added.

Split the dough into halves, wrap the halves in plastic and let them chill in the refrigerator for at least an hour.

Roll the chilled dough out between sheets of parchment paper so the dough is about a quarter inch thick.

Using a three inch round cookie cutter, cut out dough circles. Pick one of the circles up in the palm of your hand and place one teaspoon of date filling in the middle.

Place second disc on top and seal the edges with your fingers or the tines of a fork. Place onto the prepared baking sheet and sprinkle turbinado sugar on top.

Bake the cookies for 6 to 8 minutes, then transfer them to a cooling rack to set up.

TENDER CRISP LEMON
SUGAR COOKIE

Dough:

1 cup salted butter, softened

1 cup shortening

1 cup powdered sugar

1 cup granulated sugar

2 eggs, slightly beaten

1 tsp. cream of tartar

1 tsp. baking soda

1 tsp. vanilla

½ tsp. lemon extract

1 tsp. fresh grated lemon zest

4 cups all-purpose flour

Drizzle:

2 cups powdered sugar

3-5 Tbsp. heavy cream or whole milk

1 tsp. fresh grated lemon zest

coarse sugar for sprinkling, optional

Preheat oven to 375 degrees and line a baking sheet with a non-stick baking mat.

Cream together shortenings, eggs, sugar and powdered sugar. Add cream of tartar, baking soda, vanilla, lemon extract and lemon zest, then mix again.

Split the dough into halves, wrap the halves in plastic and let them chill in the refrigerator for at least thirty minutes.

Roll spoonfuls of dough into balls, then press them onto the prepared baking sheet. Bake for 10 to 12 minutes or until cookies are golden brown around the edges.

Carefully transfer the cookies from the baking sheet to a cooling rack.

While cookies are cooling, whisk powdered sugar, heavy cream or milk and zest together in a small bowl until smooth.

Pour drizzle over cooled cookies then sprinkle with coarse sugar. Allow the cookies to sit for at least thirty minutes so the drizzle sets up.

CHOCOLATE PRETZEL *with* PEANUT BUTTER

½ cup salted butter, softened

¼ cup peanut butter, melted

1 cup packed brown sugar

½ cup granulated sugar

1 egg

¼ cup whole milk

1 tsp. vanilla

1 tsp. baking soda

¼ tsp. salt

2 cup all-purpose flour

1 cup semi-sweet chocolate chips

½ cup peanut butter chips

20 to 25 pretzels broken into pieces

½ cup mini chocolate chips (optional)

Place your oven rack in the lowest position and preheat to 350 degrees. Then coat a large cast-iron skillet or 3 to 4 mini skillets with non-stick spray.

With an electric mixer, cream together the butters, sugars, egg and vanilla, scraping the sides and bottom of the bowl as needed. Reduce the speed and carefully add flour, milk, salt and baking soda, beating just until smooth.

Gently fold in chocolate chips, peanut butter chips and pretzels and press dough into your skillet with damp hands.

Bake for 30 to 35 minutes (20 minutes for mini skillets) or until cookie is lightly browned.

Transfer to wire racks to cool slightly. Top with chocolate sauce recipe, optional (pg. 121).

APPLE + BUTTERSCOTCH
SKILLET

½ cup salted butter, softened

½ cup brown sugar

½ cup granulated sugar

1 egg

2 tsp. vanilla

1 cup all–purpose flour

½ tsp. salt

¾ tsp. baking powder

½ cup old–fashioned oats

2 cups diced apples (mildly tart)

1 cup butterscotch chips

Place your oven rack in the lowest position and preheat to 350 degrees. Then coat a large cast–iron skillet or 3 to 4 mini skillets with non–stick spray.

With an electric mixer, cream together the butter, sugars, egg and vanilla.

In a separate bowl, whisk together the flour, salt, baking powder, and oats.

Pour dry ingredients into the wet ingredients and mix well. Gently fold in diced apples and butterscotch chips by hand.

Pour ingredients into skillet and pat the dough down with damp hands (to keep dough from sticking).

Bake for 25 to 35 minutes, (15 to 20 minutes for mini skillets) or until edges are browned and the center comes out clean when pricked with a tooth pick.

Allow to cool for about 20 minutes before serving. Best served with homemade salted caramel sauce recipe, optional (pg. 120) and/or vanilla ice cream.

CAMPFIRE S'MORES
SKILLET

1 cup salted butter, softened
¾ cup granulated sugar
¾ cup brown sugar, softened
2 eggs
1 tsp. baking soda
pinch of salt
2 tsp. vanilla
2¼ cups all-purpose flour
12 to 16 Hershey's kisses
1 cup semi-sweet chocolate chips
2½ cups small marshmallows

Place your oven rack in the lowest position and preheat to 350 degrees. Then coat a large cast-iron skillet or 3 to 4 mini skillets with non-stick spray.

With an electric mixer, cream together the butter, sugars, egg and vanilla, scraping the sides and bottom of the bowl as needed. Reduce the speed and carefully add flour, salt and baking soda, beating just until smooth.

Gently fold in chocolate chips and half of the marshmallows, then press dough into your skillet with damp hands.

Bake the skillet for 7 to 8 minutes. Remove it from oven and top with Hershey's kisses and remaining marshmallows.

Return skillet to the oven and bake for another 7 to 8 minutes or until cookie is lightly browned.

Mini skillets will only bake for about 10 to 12 minutes total. Take the minis out half way through to sprinkle with kisses and marshmallows, then return to the oven to finish baking time.

Transfer to wire racks to cool slightly before serving. Top with chocolate sauce recipe, optional (pg. 121).

PEACH + OATMEAL SKILLET

2 Tbsp. salted butter, softened

¾ cup canola oil

4 to 5 medium peaches

1¾ cups + 2 Tbsp. old–fashioned oats

1½ cups all–purpose flour

1 cup packed brown sugar

2 eggs

2 Tbsp. vanilla

+ ½ cup brown sugar (for sprinkling fruit)

¾ tsp. baking soda

¼ tsp. salt

½ cup slivered or sliced almonds

Place your oven rack in the lowest position and preheat to 350 degrees. Then coat a large cast-iron skillet or 3 to 4 mini skillets with non-stick spray.

In a small saucepan, add 1 tablespoon of butter. Add the sliced peaches, and sprinkle them with brown sugar. Cook the peaches for about 6 minutes, stirring often until the fruit and sugar carmelizes.

Remove the peaches from the heat and gently stir in the vanilla. Spoon out about 2 tablespoons of the sauce for serving after the skillet is baked. Place peaches into the skillet.

With an electric mixer add all other ingredients together and mix until smooth, then drop spoonfuls of dough over the peaches.

Bake for about 20 to 25 minutes (15 to 18 minutes for minis) and set on a wire rack to cool. Top with vanilla ice cream and the reserved butter from caramelizing the fruit.

SALTED CARAMEL +
CHOCOLATE CHUNK

½ cup unsalted butter, softened

½ cup packed brown sugar

¼ cup granulated sugar

1 egg

1 tsp. vanilla

½ tsp. baking soda

½ tsp. baking powder

¼ tsp. sea salt

1¾ cups all-purpose flour

1 cup unwrapped caramels

1 cup chopped milk chocolate bar

1 cup semi-sweet chocolate chips

flaked sea salt, for sprinkling

Preheat oven to 375 degrees and line a baking sheet with a non-stick baking mat.

Unwrap the caramels and cut them into pieces, then place them into the freezer until they are ready to be used.

With an electric mixer, cream together the butter, sugars and egg. Then add vanilla, baking soda, baking powder, salt and flour and mix well.

Take caramels out of the freezer and fold the chocolate chips, chopped bar and caramel into the dough.

Drop spoonfuls of dough onto your prepared baking sheet and sprinkle with flaked sea salt.

Bake for 11 to 13 minutes. The cookies will appear to still be soft in the center but take them out of the oven and let them continue to bake on the sheet for 5 to 10 more minutes. After that, transfer them onto a cooling rack.

NUTELLA + CHOCOLATE CHIP

½ cup salted butter, softened
¾ cup brown sugar
½ cup granulated sugar
1 egg + 1 egg yolk
1 tsp. vanilla
½ cup Nutella
2½ cups all—purpose flour
1 tsp. baking soda
1 tsp. cornstarch
½ tsp. salt
1¼ cups semi—sweet chocolate chips
sea salt for sprinkling, optional

Preheat oven to 350 degrees and line a baking sheet with a non-stick baking mat.

With an electric mixer, cream together butter, brown sugar and granulated sugar, then beat in egg, egg yolk, vanilla and Nutella until combined.

Add in baking soda, salt, cornstarch and flour, mix again and then gently fold in chocolate chips.

Scoop large spoonfuls of dough onto the prepared baking sheet.

Bake the cookies for 10 to 12 minutes. Allow to cool for 5 minutes on the cookie sheet, then transfer to a cooling rack and sprinkle flaked salt.

CHOCOLATE GANACHE
with TOASTED PISTACHIOS

Dough:
6 Tbsp. salted butter, softened
1 cup granulated sugar
3 eggs
2 cups bittersweet chocolate chips/chunks
2 cups semi-sweet chocolate chips
½ tsp. baking powder
½ cup all-purpose flour

Chocolate Ganache:
1 cup semi-sweet chocolate chips
¾ cup heavy whipping cream

Topping:
1 cup shelled pistachios, roughly chopped

Preheat oven to 375 degrees and line a baking sheet with a non-stick baking mat.

In a microwave safe bowl melt butter and bitter sweet chocolate chips together, checking every thirty seconds and stirring until melted.

With an electric mixer, beat eggs and sugar, then stir in the melted chocolate. Carefully add in dry ingredients and fold in semi-sweet chocolate chips by hand. Cover the dough with plastic wrap and refrigerate for about an hour.

Spoon one inch balls of chilled dough onto the baking sheet and bake for 12 to 14 minutes. Let the cookies cool for 5 minutes then transfer them from the sheet to a cooling rack.

To make the ganache, place chocolate chips in a small bowl. In a small saucepan, bring cream just to a boil. Pour the cream over the chocolate and whisk until smooth.

While ganache is cooling, take one cup of shelled pistachios, roughly chop them and place onto a clean baking sheet, (spread evenly so they are not overlapping).

Bake in the oven at same temperature, 375 degrees, for about 5 to 8 minutes.

Let the ganache cool slightly and dip cookies half way or drizzle ganache over the entire cookie and sprinkle with pistachios.

CHOCOLATE TURTLES

Dough:
½ cup salted butter, softened
½ cup granulated sugar
½ cup packed brown sugar
1 egg
1 tsp. vanilla
2 Tbsp. milk
½ cup + 2 Tbsp. cocoa powder
1 cup all-purpose flour
1 tsp. baking soda
pinch of salt

Topping:
¾ cup chopped pecans
salted caramel recipe (pg. 120)

Preheat oven to 350 degrees and line a baking sheet with a non-stick baking mat.

With an electric mixer, cream together butter, sugars, cocoa powder, egg and then add the milk. Add the rest of the dry ingredients to the wet ingredients and blend well.

Cover dough with plastic wrap and refrigerate for at least one hour.

Scoop out small spoonfuls of the chilled dough and roll into balls. Then roll each ball in chopped pecans and place onto the prepared baking sheet.

Bake the cookies for 10 to 12 minutes. Allow to cool for 5 minutes on the cookie sheet, then transfer to a cooling rack and drizzle with salted caramel sauce.

NO BAKE SNOWBALLS

½ cup salted butter, softened
1 cup granulated sugar
3 cups old-fashioned rolled oats
3 cups sweetened shredded coconut
(this will be divided in the recipe)
½ cup milk
5 Tbsp. natural cocoa powder
1 tsp. vanilla
pinch of salt

Line two baking sheets with non-stick baking mats.

Place the oats and one cup of shredded coconut in a large bowl and set aside.

Combine the butter, sugar, milk, cocoa powder, and salt together in a large saucepan over medium heat.

Whisk until the butter melts, then bring it to a boil. Remove from heat and stir in vanilla extract, then pour over the oat and coconut mixture. Stir until combined.

Cover mixture with plastic wrap and let chill in the refrigerator for at least 45 minutes to an hour.

Meanwhile, pulse the remaining coconut in a food processor and pour it into a shallow bowl.

Take spoonfuls of the chilled mixture (it will be sticky) and form into balls, then roll each ball into the broken down coconut and place onto the baking sheet.

Place baking sheets in the refrigerator for two hours to set up before serving.

CHOCOLATE CHIP KAHLÚA

1 cup salted butter, softened
¾ cup granulated sugar
¾ cup packed brown sugar
1 tsp. vanilla
1 Tbsp. Kahlúa
2 eggs
1 tsp. baking soda
1 tsp. salt
1 tsp. cinnamon
½ Tbsp. instant espresso powder
2¼ cups all-purpose flour
2 cups semi-sweet chocolate chips
or chunks (or a combination of both)

Preheat oven to 375 degrees and line a baking sheet with a non-stick baking mat.

Combine flour, baking soda, salt, cinnamon and espresso powder in a small bowl.

With an electric mixer, beat butter, sugars, vanilla extract and Kahlúa until creamy.

Add in eggs, one at a time, beating well after each addition. Gradually beat in flour mixture.

Gently stir in chocolate chips and drop rounded spoonfuls of dough onto the prepared baking sheet.

Bake for 9 to 11 minutes and allow cookies to cool on the baking sheet for 5 more minutes after removing them from the oven. Then transfer the cookies to a cooling rack.

CHOCOLATE CHIP + POTATO CHIP

1 cup salted butter, softened

½ cup granulated sugar

½ cup packed brown sugar

2 eggs

2 tsp. vanilla

2 cups all–purpose flour

1 tsp. baking soda

1 tsp. salt

1 cup milk chocolate chips

½ cup semi–sweet chocolate chips

5 cups crushed Lay's Ruffles Potato Chips

Preheat oven to 350 degrees and line a baking sheet with a non-stick baking mat.

With an electric mixer, cream together butter, sugar and brown sugar until light and fluffy. Add vanilla and eggs and beat on medium speed until just combined. Add the flour, baking soda and salt, then mix on low speed until just combined.

Stir in all chocolate chips and two cups of the crushed potato chips. Put the remaining three cups of crushed potato chips in a shallow bowl.

Roll the dough into 2 inch sized balls, then roll them in the remaining potato chips so they are completely coated.

Place the cookies 2 inches apart onto the prepared baking sheets and bake for 12 to 15 minutes.

Carefully transfer the cookies to a wire rack to cool completely.

CHOCOLATE WHOOPIES
with BOURBON CREAM

Dough:
1 cup unsalted butter, softened
1 cup packed brown sugar
1 egg
1 tsp. vanilla
1 cup buttermilk, room temperature
½ cup cocoa powder
1 tsp. baking soda
½ tsp. baking powder
½ tsp. salt
2 cups all–purpose flour

Bourbon Buttercream:
½ cup butter, softened
2 cups powdered sugar
3½ Tbsp. heavy whipping cream
2 Tbsp. bourbon
1 tsp. vanilla

Preheat oven to 350 degrees and line a baking sheet with a non–stick baking mat.

With an electric mixer, beat the butter and brown sugar until fluffy and add the egg and vanilla.

At a low speed, beat in the dry ingredients and buttermilk in three alternating additions; scrape down the sides and bottom of the bowl as necessary.

Scoop level mounds onto the prepared baking sheet, about two inches apart. Bake for about 14 minutes.

Transfer the cookies from sheets to racks and let cool completely.

Meanwhile, for the buttercream filling, beat the butter with powdered sugar and vanilla until fluffy.

Add bourbon and then whipping cream, a little at a time. Once the desired consistency is reached, scrape the filling into a pastry bag, fitted with a large circular tip.

Pipe the filling onto one of the pies and sandwich the frosting with another pie. Refrigerate for at least thirty minutes to allow the frosting to set up.

SPICED WHOOPIES *with* MARSHMALLOW CREME

Dough:

2 cups vegetable oil

4 cups light brown sugar

4 eggs

3 tsp. vanilla

1 tsp. salt

6 cups all–purpose flour

2 cups milk

2 tsp. cinnamon

1 tsp. nutmeg

2 tsp. baking soda

Filling:

3 cups powdered sugar

1 cup unsalted butter, softened

1 tsp. vanilla

½ cup marshmallow creme

3-4 Tbsp. heavy whipping cream

Preheat oven to 350 degrees and line a baking sheet with a non–stick baking mat.

With an electric mixer, beat the butter and brown sugar until fluffy and add the eggs and vanilla.

At a low speed, beat in the dry ingredients and milk in three alternating additions; scrape down the sides and bottom of the bowl as necessary.

Scoop level mounds onto the prepared baking sheet, about two inches apart. Bake for about 12 to 14 minutes.

Transfer the cookies from sheets to racks and let cool completely.

For the buttercream filling, beat the butter with powdered sugar, marshmallow creme and vanilla until fluffy. Add the whipping cream in slowly until the desired consistency is reached. Scrape the filling into a pastry bag, fitted with a large circular tip.

Pipe the filling onto one of the cookies and sandwich the frosting with another. Refrigerate for at least thirty minutes to allow the frosting to set up.

HEARTY CARROT CAKE SANDWICHES

Dough:
½ cup salted butter, softened
½ cup packed brown sugar
½ cup granulated sugar
1 egg
1 tsp. vanilla
1 cup + 3 Tbsp. all-purpose flour
½ tsp. baking soda
½ tsp. baking powder
¾ tsp. ground cinnamon
¼ tsp. salt
½ cup old-fashioned oats
½ cup shredded coconut
¾ cup finely grated carrots
¼ cup finely chopped pecans, optional
1 cup toasted and chopped pecans for rolling, optional

Frosting:
½ cup cream cheese, softened
4 Tbsp. salted butter, softened
2 cups powdered sugar
¼ tsp. vanilla

Preheat oven to 350 degrees and line a baking sheet with a non-stick baking mat.

Beat butter and sugars until fluffy, then add egg and vanilla and beat to combine, scraping the bowl if necessary.

In a separate bowl, combine flour, baking soda, baking powder, cinnamon and salt. Add the flour mixture to the butter mixture and beat on low until just combined. Add the oats, coconut, grated carrot and walnuts and mix until just combined.

Place the dough in the refrigerator for 30 minutes. Scoop the dough evenly into small mounds and place a couple inches apart on the cookie sheets.

Bake for 9 to 11 minutes, until golden brown and still slightly soft in the center. Remove from oven and transfer directly onto a cooling rack.

To make the frosting, beat cream cheese and butter until combined, then add powdered sugar and vanilla extract. Beat for a couple more minutes until smooth and spread frosting on one half of the cookie and top with another cookie.

Once the whoopies are assembled, roll them in the toasted and chopped pecans so they stick to the exposed frosting. Then place in the refrigerator for an hour to set up.

MEYER LEMON WHOOPIES

Dough:
½ cup shortening
1 cup granulated sugar
1 egg
1 tsp. vanilla
½ cup buttermilk
¼ cup warm water
juice and zest of 2 Meyer lemons
2½ cups all–purpose flour
1 tsp. baking soda
½ tsp. salt

Lemon Cream Cheese Frosting;
1 cup cream cheese, softened
½ cup salted butter, softened
3 cups powdered sugar
1 tsp. lemon extract

Preheat oven to 375 degrees and line a baking sheet with a non–stick baking mat.

With an electric mixer, fitted with the paddle attachment, cream together the shortening and sugar until light and fluffy.

Add in the egg, vanilla, buttermilk, water, lemon juice and lemon zest and mix until the ingredients are fully incorporated.

Slowly add the dry ingredients to the wet mixture and mix on medium-low speed until just combined.

Drop spoonfuls of dough/batter onto prepared cookie sheets about 2 inches apart. Bake for 6 to 7 minutes or until the edges begin to brown.

Allow cakes to cool on baking sheets for 5 minutes then transfer to wire racks to cool completely.

With an electric mixer, beat the cream cheese and butter together on high speed until smooth and creamy and add powdered sugar, vanilla, and salt—mix again.

Spread frosting on one half of the cookie and top with another cookie.

Once the whoopies are assembled, roll them in them in sprinkles or coarse sugar. Then place in the refrigerator for an hour to set up.

HOMEMADE OREOS

Dough:
½ cup + 2 Tbsp. salted butter, softened
1 cup granulated sugar
1 egg
½ cup cocoa powder
1 tsp. baking soda
¼ tsp. baking powder
¼ tsp. salt
1¼ cups all–purpose flour
sugar for rolling dough (optional)

Buttercream Filling:
3 cups powdered sugar
1 cup unsalted butter, softened
1 tsp. vanilla
3-4 Tbsp. heavy whipping cream

Preheat oven to 375 degrees and line a baking sheet with a non–stick baking mat.

With an electric mixer, cream together butter, sugar and egg. Add the rest of the dry ingredients and mix together.

Take small spoonfuls of the dough, roll them into balls and then roll in sugar to coat the exterior.

Place onto a baking sheet approximately two inches apart. With the bottom of a glass, slightly flatten the dough by pressing down lightly.

Bake for 9 minutes and transfer them to a cooling rack immediately.

To make the buttercream filling, mix butter and powdered sugar together with an electric mixer, fitted with a paddle attachment.

Mix on low speed until well blended and then increase speed to medium and beat for another 3 minutes. Add vanilla and cream and continue to beat on medium speed until frosting is fluffy.

To assemble the cookies, take a pastry bag with a larger round tip and pipe the cream into the center of one cookie (or spread filling with a butter knife or spoon). Place another cookie on top and gently press on the cookies to spread the frosting slightly.

Refrigerate for 20 minutes to allow the frosting to set up.

PB+J'S

Dough:

2 cups crisco shortening

2 cups creamy peanut butter

2 cups granulated sugar

2 cups packed brown sugar

4 eggs

2 tsp. cream of tartar

2 tsp. baking soda
dissolved in 2 Tbsp. water

1 tsp. salt

5 cups all-purpose flour

Filling:

1 cup salted butter, softened

½ cup creamy peanut butter

4 cups powdered sugar

2 tsp. vanilla

pinch of salt

3 Tbsp. whipping cream

your favorite jam or jelly (optional)

Preheat oven to 350 degrees and line a baking sheet with a non-stick baking mat.

Cream together sugars, shortening and eggs. Add remaining dough ingredients and mix well.

Roll into one and a half inch sized balls and place onto prepared cookie sheets.

Flatten down with the palm of your hand and use the tines of a fork to make the criss cross indentations.

Sprinkle each cookie with granulated sugar. Bake about 10 to 12 minutes.

Transfer cookies immediately from baking sheet to a cooling rack and make the peanut butter buttercream filling.

Cream together butter, peanut butter, powdered sugar, vanilla and salt.

Incorporate the whipping cream, one tablespoon at a time until desired consistency is reached. Then beat for five minutes until light and fluffy.

Take one cooled cookie and spread the peanut butter buttercream first. Then add jelly, bananas and/or honey and top with the second cookie.

ORANGE SUGARS *with*
CHOCOLATE GANACHE

Dough:

1 cup salted butter, softened

¾ cup powdered sugar

1½ Tbsp. orange zest (about 1 orange)

1 egg + 1 egg yolk

1½ tsp. vanilla

2 cups all–purpose flour

(plus more as needed for rolling)

Chocolate Ganache:

½ cup heavy whipping cream

½ cup semi–sweet chocolate chips

Preheat oven to 350 degrees and line a baking sheet with a non-stick baking mat.

Cream together butter, powdered sugar and orange zest, then beat until combined.

Add the egg, egg yolk and vanilla and beat on high speed until combined, scraping down the sides and up the bottom of the bowl as needed.

Add flour and mix again slowly; dough will be very soft. Wrap dough in plastic wrap and refrigerate for at least two hours.

Once dough has chilled, transfer it to a lightly floured surface, and roll out dough to half an inch thick.

Use circle cookie cutter and cut out discs, then place them two inches apart onto prepared baking sheets.

Bake cookies for about 9 to 10 minutes or just until the cookies start to brown on the edges. Transfer cookies from baking sheet to cooling rack.

To make the ganache, heat the cream in a small saucepan until it begins to gently simmer and remove from heat immediately. Add chocolate chips and whisk in ingredients until smooth. Allow to cool and thicken for at least 30 minutes.

Spread the ganache onto the flat side of one cookie and sandwich with the other. Repeat with remaining and refrigerate to let the sandwiches set up.

CRANBERRY + ORANGE + WHITE CHOCOLATE CHIP

½ cup salted butter, softened
½ cup granulated sugar
½ cup packed brown sugar
1 egg
2 Tbsp. heavy cream
1½ tsp. vanilla
1¾ cups all–purpose flour
1 tsp. baking soda
¼ tsp. salt
1 cup dried cranberries
½ Tbsp. orange zest
1 cup white chocolate chips

Preheat oven to 350 degrees and line a baking sheet with a non–stick baking mat.

Using an electric mixer, combine butter, sugars, egg, cream and vanilla and orange zest. Add in baking soda, salt and flour and mix again until all ingredients are evenly incorporated.

Drop large spoonfuls of dough onto the prepared baking sheet and bake for 8 to 10 minutes.

Remove cookies from the oven and transfer them directly to cooling racks.

CHEESECAKE STUFFED PUMPKIN DOODLES

Dough:
1 cup unsalted butter, softened
1 cup granulated sugar
½ cup packed brown sugar
¾ cup canned pumpkin puree
1 egg
2 tsp. vanilla
1½ tsp. baking powder
½ tsp. salt
½ tsp. ground cinnamon
¼ tsp. freshly ground nutmeg
3¾ cups all-purpose flour

Cheesecake Filling:
8 oz. cream cheese, softened
¼ cup granulated sugar
2 tsp. vanilla

Sugar + Spice Coating:
½ cup granulated sugar
1 tsp. ground cinnamon
½ tsp. ground ginger
dash of allspice

Preheat oven to 350 degrees and line a baking sheet with a non-stick baking mat.

To make the dough, whisk together flour, baking powder, salt, cinnamon, and nutmeg and set aside.

With an electric mixer, beat together the butter and sugars on medium speed until light and fluffy.

Blend in the pumpkin puree and beat in egg and vanilla until incorporated. With the mixer on low speed, slowly add in the dry ingredients and mix lightly. Cover and chill the dough for at least one hour.

While the dough chills, make the filling. In a small bowl, mix together the cream cheese, sugar, and vanilla until smooth and creamy. Cover and chill for at least thirty minutes.

In a small bowl, mix together the sugar and spices for the coating. Take one tablespoon of dough and flatten it into a pancake shape. Place one teaspoon of the cream cheese mixture in the middle of the pancake.

Form another tablespoon of dough into an equally sized pancake shape, and place on top, keeping the cream cheese in the middle. Gently pinch together the edges of the dough around the cream cheese to seal, then gently roll into a ball.

Roll the ball in the cinnamon-sugar mixture to coat and place on the prepared baking sheet. Bake the cookies for 10 to 15 minutes, or until they are slightly firm to the touch and the tops begin to crack.

Remove the cookies from the baking sheet immediately and let them cool on a wire rack for at least 20 minutes.

SUGAR COOKIES *with*
BUTTERCREAM FROSTING

Dough:
1 cup butter, softened
1 ½ cups granulated sugar
1 egg
1 tsp. vanilla
1 tsp. baking soda
½ tsp. baking powder
2¾ cups all–purpose flour

Frosting:
3 cups powdered sugar
1 cup butter
1 tsp. vanilla
1-2 Tbsp. heavy whipping cream

Preheat oven to 375 degrees and line a baking sheet with a non–stick baking mat.

Cream together sugar, egg and butter together until smooth. Add dry ingredients to the wet mixture and blend together.

Split dough into halves and wrap each of the halves in plastic wrap to keep soft.

Set up your working surface and dust with flour. Unwrap one of the discs and roll it out, sprinkling flour over the surface as you work to keep it from sticking to the rolling pin.

Cut out shapes and place onto a baking sheet, then refrigerate or freeze for twenty minutes. Once the dough cutouts have chilled, put them directly into the oven and bake for 9 to 11 minutes.

Let the cookies sit on the baking sheet for one to two minutes to set, then carefully remove and place onto cooling rack.

For the frosting, mix butter and vanilla together with an electric mixer and paddle attachment. Slowly add in powdered sugar. Then add whipping cream until desired consistency is reached. Beat on high speed for one to two minutes.

Frost each cookie and add sprinkles. Food coloring may be added to frosting; just add one or two drops at a time and mix until the color is even.

CHOCOLATE LINZERS *with* DULCE DE LECHE

Dough:
¾ cup almonds
½ cup dark brown sugar
1 cup unsalted butter, softened
1 egg
1 tsp. vanilla
½ tsp. baking powder
½ tsp. salt
¾ cup cocoa powder
2½ cups flour

Dulce de Leche:
1 can sweetened condensed milk

Toast almonds in a small dry skillet over medium-high heat. Cook, stirring often, until they turn golden brown and smell nutty. Rub the almonds in a kitchen towel to remove any loose skins, then transfer to a food processor.

Pulse the almonds and ¼ cup of the brown sugar in a food processor until finely ground and sandy.

In the bowl of a stand mixer, cream the butter and remaining ¼ cup brown sugar until light and fluffy, about 3 minutes. Add in the nut mixture and beat a minute longer. Scrape down the bowl and beat in the vanilla and egg until well combined.

Combine the dry ingredients in a separate bowl. Add the dry ingredients to the mixer and mix on low until just combined. Form the dough into a ball and flatten into a disc. Wrap the disc in plastic wrap and place in the freezer for 20 minutes.

Preheat oven to 350 degrees. Line a baking sheet with a non-stick baking mat.

Roll out the chilled dough on a well floured surface to ¼ inch thick. Using a cookie cutter, cut out as many cookies as you can and transfer to the prepared baking sheet. Using a smaller round cutter, or any shape you choose, cut out the center of half of the cookies. Bake 10 to 12 minutes.

To make the dulce de leche, peel the label off the can of sweetened condensed milk, place it in a pot or large saucepan, and cover it with water by 1 to 2 inches. Bring it to a very gentle boil, then reduce the heat to low and simmer. It is very important to watch the water level and add water if the level of water falls below the top of the can.

Let the can simmer for 3 hours for a dark and very flavorful sauce. After simmering, turn off the heat and allow the can to come back to room temperature. Do NOT open the can while hot!

Spread a spoonful of dulce de leche on the bottom side of a whole cookie. Sandwich together with a cut out cookie.

Finish with a dusting of powdered sugar or cinnamon.

CHOCOLATE WAFFLE IRON COOKIES

Dough:
½ cup salted butter, melted
¾ cup granulated sugar
2 eggs
1 tsp. vanilla
1 cup all-purpose flour
4½ tsp. cocoa powder

Topping:
chocolate sauce recipe (pg.121) or
chocolate espresso sauce (pg.121)
crushed candy cane, optional
chocolate sprinkles, optional

With an electric mixer, combine sugar, butter, eggs and vanilla. Carefully add cocoa powder and flour to the wet mixture and blend all ingredients thoroughly.

Drop tablespoonfuls of runny dough into each section of a preheated waffle iron. Bake about 3 minutes (each waffle iron is a little different; follow user manual for specific times and use nonstick spray if recommended on instructions). You want them to be crunchy, not doughy like a waffle.

Gently lift the cookie off the iron and immediately top with chocolate sauce and candy cane pieces or chocolate sprinkles.

SCANDINAVIAN ALMOND COOKIES

Dough:
½ cup salted butter, softened
1 cup granulated sugar
1 egg
½ tsp. almond extract
1¾ cups all-purpose flour
2 tsp. baking powder
¼ tsp. salt
½ cup sliced almonds
2 Tbsp. whole milk

Icing:
1 cup powdered sugar
¼ tsp. almond extract
¼ cup whole milk

Preheat oven to 325 degrees and line a baking sheet with a non-stick baking mat.

With an electric mixer, cream butter and sugar. Add egg and almond extract and mix well.

Add flour, baking powder and salt and mix again until ingredients are all incorporated.

Divide dough into four pieces, and roll each one into a log about twelve inches long. Place two logs onto the prepared baking sheet, four inches apart.

Flatten each roll by hand until it is about three inches wide. Brush flattened roll with milk and sprinkle with sliced almonds.

Bake for 12 to 15 minutes or until edges are slightly browned. While the cookies are still warm, cut them crosswise at a diagonal, into slices about two inches wide. Remove from cookie sheet and place on a cooling rack.

For icing, whisk together powdered sugar, almond extract, and milk until smooth. Drizzle over the cookies and sprinkle with extra almonds if desired.

ANGEL FOOD COOKIES

1 cup shortening

½ cup brown sugar

½ cup granulated sugar

1 egg

¼ tsp. salt

1 tsp. baking soda

1 tsp. cream of tartar

1 tsp. vanilla

2 cups all–purpose flour

1 cup flaked coconut

+ ¼ cup (for sprinkling)

½ cup white sugar

(for sprinkling)

Preheat oven to 375 degrees and line a baking sheet with a non-stick baking mat.

With an electric mixer, cream together shortening, sugars and egg, then add the rest of the ingredients and mix together well.

Roll the dough into one inch sized balls, then roll in coconut and place onto prepared the baking sheet. Pat each ball down to a thick disc and sprinkle with sugar.

Bake for 15 minutes and until golden brown and transfer cookies from baking sheet to a cooling rack.

PEANUT BUTTER BLOSSOMS

Dough:
½ cup butter, softened
½ cup granulated sugar
½ cup packed brown sugar
½ cup creamy peanut butter
1 egg
½ cup whole milk
1½ cups all-purpose flour
¾ tsp. baking soda
½ tsp. baking powder
granulated sugar for rolling
one small bag of Hershey's kisses

Drizzle option :
1 cup butterscotch chips
1 cup semi-sweet chocolate chips

Drizzle option:
1 cup white chocolate chips
½ cup peanut butter chips

Preheat oven to 375 degrees and line a baking sheet with a non-stick baking mat.

With an electric mixer, beat butter, sugars, peanut butter, egg and milk together.

Add in flour, baking soda and baking powder; mix again until dough forms.

Shape dough into two inch balls and roll them in extra sugar. Place the dough balls onto the prepared baking sheet and bake for 8 to 10 minutes or until edges are golden brown.

Immediately press a chocolate kiss into the center of each cookie and transfer them to a cooling rack.

While the cookies cool, choose a drizzle option and place the chocolate chips into a microwave safe bowl. Heat the chips for only 30 seconds at a time and stir in between warming.

Once the chocolate has melted, take a spoonful, drizzle the cookies, and let the chocolate set up about thirty minutes.

GINGER MOLASSES

1½ cups canola oil
2 cups granulated sugar
2 large eggs
½ cup molasses
4 tsp. baking soda
3 tsp. fresh ground ginger
or ginger paste
2 tsp. ground cinnamon
1 tsp. salt
4 cups all-purpose flour
additional sugar for rolling

Preheat oven to 350 degrees and line a baking sheet with a non-stick baking mat.

Using an electric mixer, combine sugar and oil. Beat in eggs. Stir in molasses.

Whisk the flour, baking soda, ginger, cinnamon and salt together in a bowl; gradually add them to creamed mixture and mix well.

Shape into one inch sized balls, roll in sugar and place onto baking sheet.

Bake for 10 to 12 minutes or until cookie springs back when touched lightly.

Let cookies cool on baking sheet for a couple minutes to set up slightly, then transfer to a cooling rack.

PEPPERMINT CRACKLES

½ cup sugar
2 Tbsp. canola oil
¼ cup semi–sweet chocolate chips
(melted and cooled)
½ tsp. vanilla
1 egg
½ cup all–purpose flour
½ tsp. baking powder
½ tsp. peppermint extract
dash of salt
¼ cup crushed candy cane, optional
powdered sugar to roll and dust

Preheat oven to 350 degrees and line a baking sheet with a non–stick baking mat.

With an electric mixer, beat sugar, oil, chocolate, egg, peppermint and vanilla until blended. Then mix in the dry ingredients except for the powdered sugar. The crushed candy cane may be added at this point.

Refrigerate dough, covered, for two hours or until firm enough to handle.

With powder sugared hands, shape dough into one inch sized balls then roll in powdered sugar.

Place dough balls two inches apart on baking sheets and bake 10 to 12 minutes or until they have set up slightly. Transfer the cookies from the baking sheet to a cooling rack.

SPICY GINGERBREAD

Dough:
½ cup unsalted butter, softened
¼ cup + 1 Tbsp. packed brown sugar
1 egg
½ cup molasses
½ tsp. baking soda
¼ tsp. baking powder
2 tsp. ground ginger
1½ tsp. cinnamon
1 tsp. salt
¾ tsp. ground cloves
¼ tsp. ground black pepper
2¾ cups all-purpose flour

Decorating Frosting:
1 large egg white
1 cup powdered sugar
½ Tbsp. water

Preheat oven to 325 degrees and line a baking sheet with a non-stick baking mat.

In a mixer fitted with the paddle attachment, beat the butter with the brown sugar at medium speed until fluffy, about two minutes.

Beat in ginger, cinnamon, salt, cloves and black pepper, then beat in the whole egg. With the mixer on, drizzle in the molasses and beat until blended. Add in dry ingredients and mix again.

Divide the dough in half and form into discs. Wrap each disc in plastic wrap and refrigerate until well chilled, about two hours.

On a lightly floured work surface, roll out the dough to an inch thickness. Using cookie cutters, cut the dough into shapes and transfer to the prepared baking sheets. Roll the dough scraps and repeat.

Bake the cookies for 8 to 10 minutes, until the tops are dry and the edges just start to darken. Let the cookies cool on the sheet for five minutes, then transfer to racks to cool completely.

With an electric mixer and whisk attachment, beat the egg white at medium speed until foamy. Add powdered sugar until ingredients are completely incorporated. Add a half tablespoon of water and beat at high speed until the icing holds its shape, about five minutes.

Decorate the cooled cookies with the icing and sprinkles, then serve.

EGGNOG COOKIES

Dough:
1 cup butter, softened
1 cup granulated sugar
1 egg
2 tsp. vanilla
1 tsp. baking powder
1 tsp. baking soda
½ tsp. salt
½ tsp. ground cinnamon
½ tsp. ground nutmeg
¾ cup eggnog
2½ cups all–purpose flour

Frosting:
¼ cup salted butter, softened
1½ cups powdered sugar
¼ tsp. nutmeg
1-3 Tbsp. eggnog
cinnamon and nutmeg (for sprinkling)

Preheat oven to 325 degrees and line a baking sheet with a non–stick baking mat.

With an electric mixer, combine the butter and sugar and beat on medium-high speed until well combined, about 1 to 2 minutes.

Add egg and vanilla, mixing until combined. Add baking powder, baking soda, salt, cinnamon and nutmeg, mix until combined. Carefully add eggnog and flour and blend.

Drop by spoonfuls onto the prepared baking sheet and bake for 9 to 10 minutes or until golden brown. Transfer cookies to a cooling rack and make frosting.

Beat the butter until smooth and creamy. Add powdered sugar, nutmeg and eggnog, mixing until light & fluffy (if it's too thick, add a little bit more eggnog until desired consistency is reached; or if it's too thin, add more powdered sugar.)

Spread frosting on each cookie and sprinkle with cinnamon.

RED VELVET

½ cup salted butter, softened

1 cup granulated sugar

1 tsp. distilled white vinegar

1 egg

1½ tsp. vanilla

1½ tsp. red food coloring (tasteless)

1½ cups all-purpose flour

2½ Tbsp. cocoa powder

1 tsp. cornstarch

¾ tsp. baking powder

¼ tsp. salt

¾ cup white chocolate chips

Preheat oven to 375 degrees and line a baking sheet with a non-stick baking mat.

With an electric mixer, beat together butter, sugar and vinegar until pale and fluffy, then mix in egg.

Add in vanilla and red food coloring and mix until blended. With mixer set on low speed, slowly add in dry ingredients and mix just until combined.

Gently fold in white chocolate chips by hand. Scoop dough out by the heaping spoonfuls and shape into balls and place onto prepared baking sheet.

Bake for 9 to 11 minutes. Carefully transfer cookies to a cooling rack.

BROWN SUGAR SHORTIES

1 ¼ cup salted butter, softened
½ cup packed brown sugar
2 ¼ cups all–purpose flour
¼ tsp. ground cinnamon
¼ tsp. ground cloves

Preheat oven to 350 degrees and line a baking sheet with a non–stick baking mat.

With an electric mixer, beat the butter until soft and smooth. Add the brown sugar, cinnamon and cloves and mix until incorporated.

Add flour to the butter mixture and mix at low speed just until the ingredients are incorporated and the dough comes together.

Move dough onto a floured surface and knead until the dough is smooth.

Wrap dough in plastic wrap and refrigerate for at least two hours.

Transfer the chilled dough to a lightly floured surface, and roll out dough to half an inch thick.

Use cookie cutter of choice and place cutouts one inch apart onto prepared baking sheets.

Bake for 15 minutes until very lightly browned. Remove from baking sheet and transfer to a cooling rack.

CHOCOLATE ESPRESSO

2 cups all-purpose flour
¾ cup cocoa powder
2 Tbsp. instant espresso powder
½ tsp. salt
½ cup plus 2 Tbsp. granulated sugar
1 cup salted butter, softened
1 tsp. vanilla

Dipping Chocolate:
2 cups semi-sweet chocolate chips, melted

Preheat oven to 350 degrees and line a baking sheet with a non-stick baking mat.

Cream the butter and sugar together with an electric mixer until light and fluffy.

Stir in the flour, salt, espresso powder and cocoa powder and beat on low speed just until blended.

Wrap dough in plastic wrap and refrigerate for at least two hours.

Transfer chilled dough to a lightly floured surface, and roll out dough to half an inch thick.

Use cookie cutter of choice and place cutouts one inch apart onto prepared baking sheets.

Bake cookies for about 15 minutes or just until the cookies look dry.

Microwave chocolate chips in 30 second intervals and stir in between. Repeat these steps until the chocolate is smooth.

When the cookies are cool, dip them into melted chocolate. Add sprinkles if desired and place the cookies on wax paper until the chocolate has completely

LAVENDER THINS

1 cup salted butter, softened
2 cups all–purpose flour
½ cup granulated sugar
pinch of salt
2 Tbsp. dried lavender

Preheat oven to 350 degrees and line a baking sheet with a non-stick baking mat.

Cream the butter and sugar together with an electric mixer until light and fluffy.

Stir in flour, salt, and lavender and beat on low speed just until blended.

Wrap dough in plastic wrap and refrigerate for at least two hours.

Transfer chilled dough to a lightly floured surface, and roll out dough to half an inch thick.

Use cookie cutter of choice and place cutouts one inch apart onto prepared baking sheets.

Bake cookies for about 18 to 20 minutes or just until they begin to color along the edges. Transfer cookies from baking sheet to cooling rack immediately.

ROSEMARY + WALNUT COOKIES

¾ cup salted butter, softened

¾ cup granulated sugar

1 Tbsp. finely chopped fresh rosemary + fresh leaves to place on sliced cookies

1 tsp. baking powder

½ tsp. freshly ground black pepper

¼ tsp. salt

1 egg

1 tsp. vanilla

2 cups all-purpose flour

¾ cup chopped toasted walnuts

Preheat oven to 375 degrees and line a baking sheet with a non-stick baking mat.

With an electric mixer, beat butter and add the next five ingredients (through salt) and beat until combined, scraping bowl as needed. Beat in egg and vanilla.

Add flour and mix carefully so all ingredients have been incorporated. Some of the toasted walnuts can be added to the dough; optional.

Divide dough in half. Shape each half into a 2 inch diameter roll. Coat roll with walnuts. Wrap each in plastic wrap or waxed paper and chill dough for one hour.

Use a serrated knife to cut rolls into quarter inch thick slices and place onto the prepared baking sheet.

Press extra fresh rosemary leaves onto the tops of the sliced cookies.

Bake 7 to 9 minutes or until bottoms are light brown. Cool cookies for a couple minutes, then remove them from the baking sheet and transfer to a cooling rack.

NO BAKE BIRD SEED MOUNDS

3 cups rolled oats
1 cup raisins or dried cranberries
(optional)
1 cup sesame seeds
1 cup sunflower seeds
1 cup pepita seeds
1 cup pure maple syrup
1 cup crunchy peanut butter
1 tsp. vanilla
¼ tsp. cinnamon
pinch of nutmeg

Line a baking sheet with parchment paper or a non-stick baking mat.

In a small saucepan over medium heat, melt peanut butter and maple syrup until the mixture turns to a thick liquid. Remove from the heat and add vanilla.

In a medium to large bowl, add all dry ingredients.

Mix liquid mixture with all of the dry ingredients so that the warmed mixture coats them evenly.

When the oats, seeds and grains have cooled, roll into 1 inch balls, place them onto a prepared cookie sheet and refrigerate or freeze to set up.

CHOCOLATE CHIP OATIES

¾ cup butter, softened

1 cup packed brown sugar

½ cup granulated sugar

1 egg

¼ cup water

1 tsp. vanilla

1 tsp. salt

½ tsp. baking soda

3½ cups quick oats

1 cup all-purpose flour

2 cups milk chocolate chips

Preheat oven to 350 degrees and line a baking sheet with a non-stick baking mat.

Blend together softened butter, sugar and egg until smooth. Add in water, vanilla, salt and baking soda and mix again.

Add flour, and oats and mix until ingredients are even. Then gently fold in chocolate chips by hand.

Drop spoonfuls of dough onto prepared baking sheet and bake for 12 minutes or until cookies are golden brown.

Remove cookies from the oven and place them onto a cooling rack.

CARAMELIZED APPLE OATMEAL

Caramelized Apple:

3 medium apples peeled and diced
(Fuji or Honeycrisp)

2 Tbsp. salted butter, softened

4 tsp. packed brown sugar

Dough:

¾ cup salted butter, softened

¾ cup brown sugar,packed

¼ cup granulated sugar

1 tsp. baking soda

1½ tsp. cinnamon

½ tsp. salt

¼ cup apple sauce

2½ tsp. vanilla

2 eggs

3 cups rolled oats

1½ cups all-purpose flour

Glaze:

1 cup powdered sugar

1 Tbsp. water

To caramelize the apples, cook the butter, sugar and diced apples, in a saucepan over medium heat until sugar has dissolved and begins to turn a deep amber color. Set aside to cool.

Preheat oven to 350 degrees and line a baking sheet with a non-stick baking mat.

Cream together the butter and sugars until light and fluffy. Add the eggs, one at a time, mixing well after each addition. Add the apple sauce and vanilla and beat on high for a minute.

Add in dry ingredients and mix again until just combined.

Gently fold in the cooled caramelized apples, being careful not to over mix. Cover the mixing bowl with plastic wrap or a piece of foil and refrigerate for at least one hour.

Take rounded spoonfuls of chilled dough and place them onto the baking sheet. Bake cookies for 15 to 18 minutes, or until edges are just starting to brown.

Remove baking sheet from the oven and allow cookies to cool for at least 5 minutes before transferring to a cooling rack to cool completely.

In a small bowl whisk together the sugar and water. If glaze is too thick add additional water, (just a couple drops); if it's too watery, add additional powdered sugar. Drizzle glaze over the tops of each cookie using a spoon.

JUMBO SALTED
PEANUT COOKIE

½ cup butter, softened

1¼ cup crunchy peanut butter

1¼ cup sugar + 3 Tbsp., divided

5 egg whites, divided

2 tsp. vanilla

2 tsp. water

1 tsp. baking soda

½ tsp. salt

2 cups salted peanuts
(regular or Spanish)

1½ cups all–purpose flour

Preheat oven to 375 degrees. Line two oversized baking sheets with parchment paper. Set aside.

Place a half cup of the salted peanuts into the food processor. Add flour, baking soda and salt. Pulse until the peanuts are about a quarter inch sized pieces.

Place butter into three quart saucepan and melt slowly. Set aside. When cool, whisk in peanut butter until smooth. Stir in one and a quarter cup sugar until smooth.

Add four of the egg whites, mixing thoroughly until combined. Blend in vanilla. With a wooden spoon, stir in the dry ingredients, mixing just until combined.

Whisk remaining egg white with water into a shallow dish. Pour the remaining peanuts into a pie plate. Spoon the dough into a quarter cup measuring cup. Knock on the side of the counter to release.

Dip the top side of the dough into the egg wash mixture and then into the peanuts, covering generously. Place the dough, nut side up onto the sheet pan. Flatten down to about a three inch disc about half an inch thick.

Sprinkle the top of each cookie with a half teaspoon of sugar. Bake for 14 to 16 minutes or until the edges of the cookie are slightly brown and tops are set. Let rest on baking sheet for 5 minutes and transfer to a cooling rack.

RASPBERRY ALMOND THUMBPRINTS

5 Tbsp. butter, softened
¾ cup almond paste
¾ cup granulated sugar
¼ tsp. vanilla
1 egg white
1¼ cups all-purpose flour
¼ tsp. salt
6 Tbsp. raspberry jam

Preheat oven to 350 degrees and line a baking sheet with a non-stick baking mat.

Place first three ingredients in a bowl; beat with a mixer at medium speed until light and fluffy. Then add vanilla and egg white and beat well.

Add flour and salt to almond paste mixture and beat at a low speed until well blended. Then shape dough into one inch sized balls.

Place balls one inch apart on prepared baking sheets, and press thumb into center of each cookie.

Bake for 15 minutes or until golden brown and transfer cookies to a cooling rack.

Once the cookies have cooled, spoon the jam into the reservoirs.

ALMOND BUTTER COOKIE

1 cup natural almond butter
½ cup unsalted butter, softened
1 cup packed brown sugar
1 egg + 1 egg yolk
1 tsp. vanilla
1 tsp. baking soda
½ tsp. salt
2 cups all–purpose flour
½ cup pepita seeds
¼ cup chia seeds
2 Tbsp. flax seed, ground

Preheat oven to 375 degrees and line a baking sheet with a non-stick baking mat.

With an electric mixer, beat butter, almond butter, vanilla, egg, egg yolk and sugar together. Add the dry ingredients and mix until all ingredients are combined.

Scoop a spoonful of dough and roll into a ball, then place the dough balls onto the prepared baking sheet. Flatten slightly with the palm of your hand and make criss cross indentations with the tines of a fork, then sprinkle with sugar.

Bake for 7 to 8 minutes or until golden brown. Remove the cookies from the baking sheet immediately and transfer them to a cooling rack.

WHITE CHOCOLATE +
MACADAMIA NUT + BLUEBERRY

1 cup salted butter, softened

1½ cups granulated sugar

1 cup packed brown sugar

2 eggs

1½ tsp. vanilla

½ tsp. baking soda

1 tsp. salt

3 cups all–purpose flour

2 cups white chocolate chips

1 cup macadamia nuts, chopped

1 cup dried blueberries

Preheat oven to 350 degrees and line a baking sheet with a non–stick baking mat.

Cream together butter and sugars until fluffy. Add vanilla and eggs, one at a time and beat well after each addition. Blend in baking soda and salt, then mix in the flour.

Stir in white chocolate chips and nuts. Drop by large mounded spoonfuls onto the prepared baking sheet.

Bake 10 to 12 minutes or until the edges of the cookie become slightly brown.

Remove cookies from the baking sheet and place onto a cooling rack.

COCONUT KEY LIME

1 cup salted butter, softened

1½ cups sugar

1 egg

½ tsp. vanilla

½ tsp. salt

½ tsp. baking powder

1 tsp. baking soda

zest of one lime or 3 key limes

3 Tbsp. key lime juice

½ cup toasted coconut

2¾ cups all-purpose flour

½ cup turbinado sugar, to coat dough

Preheat oven to 350 degrees and line a baking sheet with a non-stick baking mat.

To toast coconut, place on another cookie sheet lined with a non-stick baking mat and bake at 350 degrees for 6 to 9 minutes.

Stir and flip coconut gently until it is lightly browned. Remove from the oven and set aside to cool.

In a small bowl, whisk together first four dry ingredients and set aside.

Using a mixer, beat butter and sugar together until smooth and fluffy.

Beat in the egg, vanilla, key lime juice and lime zest.

Add in dry ingredients with toasted coconut. Mix until combined but don't over mix.

Roll rounded teaspoonfuls of dough into balls. Then roll the balls in a bowl of turbinado sugar. Place on the prepared cookie sheet about two inches apart.

Bake 8 to 10 minutes or until lightly browned. Let cookies stand for a couple minutes and move to cooling rack.

TRAIL MIXERS

2 eggs
1 tsp. vanilla
1 tsp. baking powder
1 tsp. baking soda
1 cup chunky peanut butter
1 cup butter, softened
1 cup sugar
1 cup dark brown sugar
1 cup quick oats
1 cup sweetened shredded coconut
1 cup all-purpose flour
1 cup pepita seeds
1 cup sunflower seeds
1 cup sesame seeds
1 cups raisins
1 cup dried cranberries or
dried blueberries
1 cup 60% cacao chips
1 cup chopped peanuts
½ cup M&M candies

Preheat oven to 350 degrees and line a baking sheet with a non-stick baking mat.

Cream butter, peanut butter, sugars and egg together. Add in vanilla, baking powder and baking soda and mix until well blended.

Then add in all or some of the desired ingredients and spoon rounded mounds onto the prepared sheet. Bake for 13 to 15 minutes or until golden brown.

Remove cookies from the baking sheet immediately and place on a cooling rack.

SALTED CARAMEL SAUCE

1 cup granulated sugar
¼ cup water
¾ cup heavy whipping cream
3½ Tbsp. salted butter
1 tsp. flaked sea salt

In a saucepan, combine the sugar and water over medium heat until the sugar dissolves.

Increase the heat and bring to a gentle boil, without stirring. Boil until the syrup is a deep amber color, about 7 to 9 minutes.

Remove the sugar from the heat and carefully whisk in the heavy cream, butter and salt. The liquid may violently bubble and steam so use caution while adding in these ingredients.

Transfer the caramel to a mason jar or dish to cool and store.

Salted caramel should be kept in the refrigerator and lasts for 3 to 4 months.

CHOCOLATE SAUCE

½ cup + 3 Tbsp. granulated sugar
½ cup light corn syrup
1 ¼ cup heavy whipping cream
5 Tbsp. salted butter
2 cups chocolate chips
2 tsp. vanilla

In a saucepan, combine the sugar, light corn syrup and heavy whipping cream over medium heat until the sugar dissolves.

Increase the heat and bring to a gentle boil and remove the cream mixture from the heat.

Whisk in chocolate chips, butter and vanilla, then transfer the sauce to a mason jar or dish to cool and store.

Chocolate sauce should be kept in the refrigerator and lasts for 3 to 4 months.

CHOCOLATE ESPRESSO SAUCE

½ cup + 3 Tbsp. granulated sugar
½ cup light corn syrup
1 ¼ cup heavy whipping cream
5 Tbsp. salted butter
2 cups chocolate chips
2 tsp. vanilla
¼ cup fresh brewed espresso or
4 Tbsp. instant espresso powder

In a saucepan, combine the sugar, light corn syrup and heavy whipping cream over medium heat until the sugar dissolves.

Increase the heat and bring to a gentle boil and remove the cream mixture from the heat.

Whisk in chocolate chips, butter, espresso and vanilla then transfer the sauce to a mason jar or dish to cool and store.

Chocolate espresso sauce should be kept in the refrigerator and lasts for 3 to 4 months.

INDEX